KAILYN LOWRY

A POST HILL PRESS BOOK

Hustle and Heart
© 2016 by Kailyn Lowry
All Rights Reserved

ISBN: 978-1-61868-815-6
ISBN (eBook): 978-1-61868-814-9

Cover photograph by Jonpaul Brown
Interior Design and Production by Greg Johnson

Post Hill Press
posthillpress.com

Published in the United States of America
1 2 3 4 5 6 7 8 9 10

Contents

Introduction

Being in the public eye, I have received more "advice" than I would have ever imagined. Although most of it is unsolicited, and a majority of it is outrageous, I have seen some helpful tidbits throughout the years.

Whether you're finding inspiration from clever Instagram quotes and thoughtful tweets, or chatting with your lifelong girlfriends, it seems there is an endless amount of advice to go around. We all seem to give advice by the bucket and take it by the grain.

However, oftentimes the people behind these "life changing" nuggets of knowledge are also people who have never been through similar experiences whatsoever.

So what makes me more qualified than anyone else? Well. Let me acknowledge those who think I have no business giving anyone advice. Yes, I see you out there, and I'm well aware of how you feel.

Why would anyone take advice from Kailyn from Teen Mom 2?

What did she ever do except get pregnant?

The only reason we even know who she is, is because she got lucky and wound up on MTV.

How can she go out there and act like she's some kind of role model?

I could go on, but what's the point? I know some people think it's sad that I have a platform to share my thoughts and speak my mind. I happen to think it's sad that I can skim through my Instagram comments at any given moment and see so many strangers repeating the same negative comments over and over. Sure, I have lots of supporters, and I'm incredibly lucky to have so many fans from the show who have encouraged me along the way. The kindness of strangers is an amazing thing. It's a shame that the negativity sometimes stands out more.

Then, again, someone once said that a successful woman is one who can build a foundation with the bricks that have been thrown at her. So, hey. Thanks for the bricks.

And as for the idea that I shouldn't be giving anyone advice? All I can say is that I'm not trying to act like I'm smarter, wiser or more mature than anyone else. That's not why I wrote this book.

I wrote it because when I got the opportunity, I was and still am at a point in my life where I need to step back and make sense of my own story. Not to go back over what has happened—that's what the first book was for—but to underline what I've really learned from it all. Because I need those lessons now more than ever. I need to be sure of my values, my beliefs and my intentions.

Some people say life is a series of crossroads. Lately I think it's more like a series of school semesters, some of them naturally harder than others. You know you're supposed to pay attention and do your best to learn. But sometimes you get distracted, or lazy or overwhelmed. The worst times are when you're trying as hard as you can to do well, but you just can't wrap your head around the material.

Before you know it there's a final coming up. And you're suddenly facing the very real possibility that you could fail.

This isn't my first test. But it's a big one. And I *have* to pass.

My friends keep telling me I've been going against the grain lately. It seems like I'm going against the things I'm expected to want, resisting what society defines as the good life. I'm supposed to strive for the big house with the white picket fence and the perfect all-American family. Well, I have the big house. I have the picket fence.

My husband tells me he doesn't know who I am anymore. He's not wrong to think I've changed. How do you grow without changing? And wasn't I supposed to grow?

When we set long-term goals, we have no way of knowing how those goals will fit into our lives years down the line. When I had a child at age seventeen, I made it my mission to defy everyone's expectations and rise above the statistics and stigmas that are stacked against me.

Since 2010 I've been on TV, and my struggles have been my identity. Now, especially with the show coming to an end, it's time for my accomplishments to stand out. I want to show everyone that even though I grew up like white trash and got knocked up at seventeen, I can get a Bachelor's degree and raise children who blow people away with their manners, wit and intelligence.

I've poured so much passion into this mission. I've had to work my ass off. And all along the way, I've looked for ways to grow.

The cycle of life is based on growth and change. Everyone has different experiences, different lessons, different results. Even people who have goals in common don't always stay aligned in the end, even if they really, really want to be.

It's time to focus on all the ways I've grown and all the lessons I've learned. The real test is accepting change. Am I strong enough to let go of the person I was for the person I want to become? Can I be sure enough of my own truth to do what I feel is right, even if the people who love me try to talk me out of it?

As the test approaches, all I can do is review everything I've learned and share my notes with those who could use them. They say that if someone can't take their own advice, it's probably not worth listening to. Well, let's see how I do.

Have Hustle
&
Have Heart

17

1

A while back, I went to a professional event for business owners and entrepreneurs who identify as females and mothers. *Mompreneurs*, as they say in those parts. At these events, mompreneurs come together to talk about their business ventures, brainstorm ideas, collaborate and expand their networks. It always inspires me to be around people who take their goals seriously. Passion and motivation can be contagious.

At the time, I had a few big ideas I wanted to feel out. At the top of the list was writing another book. *Pride Over Pity* is one of my proudest accomplishments. Since that memoir, my life and point of view had gone through some major changes. I was at a turning point in my life where I was grappling with a lot of difficult changes and complicated questions. I'd been thinking about what it means to be happy, to be a good person, to have a successful life, and I knew there was a core truth to it all that I wanted to explore and share. It just hadn't fully taken shape yet.

It felt like a sign when I saw a flyer printed with a phrase that caught my attention: "Whatever you do in life, have hustle and have heart."

It was everything.

Hustle and heart. Those words tied together everything I wanted to explain. They summed up the core of my experiences and the force that has guided my decisions. They applied to life, business, self-esteem, relationships and everything else I could think of.

Who would have known I'd find my entire personal philosophy summed up in one sentence on a random flyer? It may sound silly, but I don't think it is. To me, it's just proof that you can find truth in unexpected places if you make a habit of keeping your eyes and ears open to the world around you.

During my junior year in college, I started carrying a notebook everywhere. I used to capture anything that caught my eye, anything that sparked a surprising feeling inside me. Things I saw and heard around me, words spoken by my friends and professors, and random thoughts that passed through my head. As I collected all these little bits and pieces, I realized what I was doing was looking for bits of wisdom. Little by little, I started to translate my observations into larger lessons and apply them to my life.

One day someone I knew in college told me that it's important to understand your surroundings, recognize things for what they are and accept reality for what it is. "But," this person added, "if you're persistent and determined enough, you can change your surroundings by opening closed doors."

After six years of being in the public eye with people watching and judging my character and my choices, I consider it crucial to be the best me that I can be and to set a good example for those who have followed my story. That doesn't mean being perfect. I wouldn't expect that of anyone, and I know better than to demand it of myself. It's okay to be human and screw up from time to time but what matters is owning up and learning from the mistakes. That's how we move forward and gain perspective and knowledge.

Life puts pressure on us in unpredictable ways. We can only deal with it as well as we can. What drives me forward is that combination of hustle and heart, and never one without the other.

Over the last couple years I've realized I am really in the guts of the television industry, where people think of me more as a character than a real person. Sometimes I scroll through comment after comment on websites and social media, amazed by this kind of alternate reality where my life and choices are up for debate, where "opinions" and "facts" are thrown around like everyone knows everything about me, but somehow they think I have no feelings.

"It comes with the territory," you might say. Maybe so, but not all of us entered that territory knowingly.

So why not get out? I'd like to think people understand that it's not that simple, but the biggest reason to stay in this strange situation is that I can't let go of the opportunity to show people a bigger picture than what they've seen. I know many of my fellow cast members would say the same thing, and they're all bringing that motivation to life in different ways through their projects and the way they present their stories and express their growth.

I know there are people out there who recognize my hustle and see how I never stop, and I look forward to sharing my accomplishments with them just as much as I look forward to proving doubters wrong with my success. By the end of 2016, I think I may be the first person in the franchise to get a Bachelor's degree. And no, I'm not saying that to rate myself higher than them. They are all doing their own things that have just as much meaning to them. But this is the dream I have wanted for myself. I wanted to defy the statistics and be able to celebrate this milestone.

It means even more to me now that I've come so far. If anything ever took hustle and heart, it was this. Hustle in that it's hard work to go through college and get a degree. Heart in that it takes a lot of inner strength to dive into a world of unfamiliar challenges and face your own shortcomings without being discouraged.

That's the essence of it. The hustle is working your ass off and never giving up on your dreams. The heart is dealing with the emotional setbacks you encounter along the way, as well as being kind to others and to yourself.

At any given moment, one half is usually harder than the other. While you're working like a crazy person, your heart might be struggling to deal with negativity in the rest of your life. Even when it seems like your hard work is starting to pay off, you might be tempted to compare yourself to other people and be heartbroken when even your successes don't measure up.

I'm not religious at all, as you know if you read my first book. But I'm not narrow-minded, either. Not long ago I went to church with some good friends of mine, carrying my notebook under my arm. Of course the pastor was speaking in religious terms, but I felt that some of the things he said applied to life in a wider sense. For example, he brought up the expression "You can't compare apples to oranges," but his view was that you actually *should* compare the two. His explanation was that God is the orange and people are the apples, and the apples have to do the right thing for God. Or something.

Okay, maybe I missed the point. But there was something in what he was saying—that there can be good reasons to compare apples and oranges for the purpose of self-improvement—that got me thinking about my own interpretation. I thought of the oranges as all the good things you want to be in life, the people you look up to. And the apples could be us, the people working hard to achieve things like those people we look up to. The point being that it's okay to compare yourself to someone different, if it helps you make a positive change.

For me, the orange is learning how to bite my tongue and show my appreciation better. People are always telling me that I can seem mean or cold and that I don't act like I appreciate things. That's not what it feels like to me at all. I feel like my intentions are good, but I'm too direct in expressing what I believe to be true, and I don't sugarcoat things as often as other people do. Maybe sometimes I get so caught up in setting goals and solving problems that I forget to let people know that I value what's in front of me.

I'm always arguing that being realistic doesn't make me negative. I try to set realistic goals and do realistic things, things that I know I can do. I try to be realistic when I look at things in general. I don't think it's smart to set your expectations unreasonably high. You're just setting yourself up to be let down. I know it doesn't sound like the most positive mindset to some people, but it is for me. It's how I make sense of the world and get things done. It's how I achieve good things.

I don't want to change who I am. But I do want to do a better job at being me. I don't want to ever lose myself in the hustle to the point where I forget how to be careful with the hearts around me.

Becoming your best self is one of the hardest challenges there is. But understanding who you are, what you believe, and what you want in life are all good steps to take in that direction.

Hustle & Heart

I don't pretend to have a perfect grasp on life. But I try to have hustle and heart in everything I do, from my long-term goals to my daily habits. I try to keep myself accountable and look for ways to grow, whether that's attending a conference for mompreneurs or carrying a notebook around so I can make the most of all those little random opportunities life gives us to learn and grow.

I guess what you're reading now is an evolution of that notebook. This is me trying to find the truths that have been forming in my brain, activate them with words and bring them into reality.

Writing is a strange and powerful thing. You can use it to capture moments and thoughts you don't want to slip away, or to vent your innermost feelings. You can write down your hopes, dreams and goals. You can organize your plans into neat lists and start chipping away at the things you need to do to achieve your goals.

When you write things down, you're bringing thoughts out of your own mind and into the world. When you put your views in print, you're making a statement that this is what you really believe.

It's a test of confidence and a test of the faith you have in what you're saying. And when you look back over it all, there's a sense of pride in seeing the vastness of the ideas you've explored and the effort you've put into making sense of your world.

What's hustle? It's working hard, making difficult choices and being ready to jump on any opportunities that come your way.

What's heart? It's being passionate in your pursuits, true to your beliefs, good to your loved ones and kind to yourself.

Life isn't always fair, but there are always ways we can improve our odds. Hustle and heart are the ingredients I count on for every kind of success I can think of, from healthy relationships to professional advancement. What more can you ask of a person than that they be hardworking and kind? What might we accomplish if we asked it of ourselves?

Loving Yourself
is a Superpower

2

Love takes many forms. There's the love of two people in a relationship, the love of a mother for her child, love between friends, loving the life you live and loving yourself.

It's this last type of love, loving yourself, that many people will try to talk you out of, whether they know they're doing it or not. Maybe this is because the more you love yourself, the less you need other people—and the less you're willing to put up with the ones who aren't good for you.

Superheroes can be intimidating. Think about your healthiest relationships. Are they based only on a sense of need? No. The healthiest relationships happen when the people in them are there by choice, not because they feel like they can't let go. If you're in a relationship based on a feeling of need, the other person might sense that if you ever found the courage to really love and respect yourself, you'd be out the door. So whether it's a deliberate effort or something more subconscious, they often find little ways to ensure this doesn't happen.

On the other hand, that might not be your problem. You might have people singing your praises all day long, but no matter what they say, you're unable to take their uplifting words as fact. It's like there's a mental block that stops you from being able to believe you are worthy of love.

Let's face it, it's a lot easier to internalize the bad things people have to say than it is to take in the good. Learning to love yourself is hard, no matter how you slice it.

For a long time I had very low self-esteem. For a variety of reasons, I struggled to believe in the possibility that I might actually be worth the love of others. It sure as hell seemed like my own parents couldn't muster up any love to send my way. My own parents! If I couldn't look to them for an example of what it means to be loved, how could I imagine what it was like? If my parents couldn't love me, how could I be sure anyone would? I certainly couldn't love myself. I was constantly nitpicking everything about myself.

Everyone can relate to feeling this way at some point or another. Maybe you still feel that way today. Unloved, or unlovable. But you don't have to settle for feeling that way. Loving yourself is a superpower, and you'll be amazed at how much of a difference it can make in your life once you harness it in a way that works for you.

We all have our own journeys when it comes to loving ourselves. What it means for me to love myself is probably vastly different from what it means to you. The journey to happiness is a personal one, filled with choices you have to make for yourself and realizations you can't explain to other people. There will always be someone looking at your journey and pointing out things you could or should have done differently. But you're the only one who can judge your happiness for yourself. And just like you can't depend on other people to direct your relationships, you can't depend on others to direct your relationship with yourself. That love affair is between you and you.

For me, loving myself is a journey that happens both inside and out. For years I struggled with eating disorders, and I was extremely self-conscious about my weight. As anyone who's been in this situation knows, this is rarely something you ever completely get over. It's nice to think that the ultimate goal would be to feel totally at peace with my body, whatever it looks like. But in reality, that's something that has to be maintained continuously. There's always another reason to take a dip in confidence, whether it's spotting your first wrinkles in the mirror or dealing with the body changes that come after having kids.

But just like in any other situation, the best thing to do is to take control. For me, that meant getting into exercise. I took up Crossfit with the hope of putting an end to my constant weight fluctuations and the turmoil that came with them. It was a great decision. The longer I stuck with it, the more reason I had to be positive and proud of my body and my relationship with it. Still, after fourteen months, I wasn't getting the specific results I was hoping for. I'd committed so thoroughly to working out and maintaining a healthy diet, but it was clear there was only so much I could do to change the shape of my body.

So, I made a choice. A choice that isn't right for everyone, but was right for me. After much thought and research, I decided to get plastic surgery.

When the news about my plastic surgery broke, social media erupted with people from all over the world spouting off their opinions about my decision. As you can imagine, most people only had negative things to say. As you can also imagine, I didn't really care. The choice to undergo plastic surgery was mine and mine alone. Haters to the left!

Guess what? I was doing *me*. I didn't make that decision under pressure. No one around me was making me feel bad about my body. I was just doing me, and if your mission is to love yourself, I would encourage you to do you.

This doesn't mean I'm advocating plastic surgery as the right decision for everyone. There are plenty of things you can do to lift your self-esteem and learn to love yourself, and it should go without saying that this goes far deeper than just loving your appearance.

My decision to get plastic surgery came down to one simple thing: I'm human. I care how I look. I knew that being satisfied with my outer appearance would give me the confidence I needed to face the world head on. For me, the things that I wanted to change about my body were nagging little distractions from the deeper missions I wanted to work on. Removing that stress from my life made more room for me to focus on my family, friends, education, and career.

Don't get it twisted, though. Loving yourself has very little to do with outer beauty at all. It's more about recognizing value in yourself and giving yourself as much credit as you give to the people you care about. What makes you feel valuable? Maybe you feel talented or skillful when you're immersed in a favorite hobby. Maybe it's being able to engage in conversations that make you feel smart. Maybe it makes you feel good to give your friends advice and know that people trust your opinions. It might give you a sense of peace and creative satisfaction to care for and decorate your living space. There are endless places to find areas in your life where you can take credit for your accomplishments and feel proud of yourself.

I love myself when I'm sitting on my couch in my PJs snuggled up with my children watching cartoons. If I looked in a mirror, would I actually appear to be my most gorgeous self? I wouldn't put it to a vote. In the long run, we all know looks are fleeting anyway. But spending time with my sons and seeing them happy, soaking up the safe and positive atmosphere that I've helped to create for them, that gives me peace and pride. Those cuddles, kisses and memories mean more than anything and last a lifetime. I never feel more beautiful in my mind, body or soul than in those mommy moments.

You can also bet that when I'm kicking ass at Crossfit, sweaty as hell, I feel damn good about myself. Maybe it's the rush of endorphins, but I think it's more than that. I've made time for myself to blow off steam while doing something that benefits my health and overall wellness. Maybe Crossfit isn't your thing, but there's a lot to be said for finding a physical activity that you're comfortable with and gets you moving. Whether it's running a few times a week or going out on foot and exploring your town, you'll have done something positive for your emotional and physical well-being, and you'll feel great. Sometimes a nice long walk is all you need to calm your nerves and reclaim your calm. I think we can all get behind that, right?

Another joy I've found in my life is being able to channel my energy into creative endeavors. Whether it's decorating my home, writing my first children's book, *Love is Bubblegum*, or working on my forthcoming coloring book for grown-ups, being able to express myself through art and writing has been empowering and fun. Everyone has at least one creative bone in their body, whether it's something like woodworking or painting, or something less obvious like rearranging your furniture or writing letters to friends. And the point isn't to be good at it. You're not doing it to impress anyone. The important thing is to give yourself a chance to express it in whatever way feels cathartic and satisfying for you.

Accepting who you are as a person, including your flaws, is a necessary component when it comes to gaining the superpower that is self-love. We all have personal obstacles when it comes to gaining compassion for ourselves. Many of us even have people in our lives who try to stand in our way. It's important to remember that the relationship you have with yourself comes first, and no one should make you feel bad about that.

I, for one, can proudly tell myself with total certainty that I'm a great mom. No one will ever be able to take that source of confidence away from me. It's something I'm proud of and I know to be true. Not just because I feel it in my heart, but because I can see that truth for myself. The evidence is in my sons' eyes, the frequency of their laughter and the comfort and confidence they show when they're with me. It's in the pleasure and surprise I see in the faces of people who meet Isaac and Lincoln for the first time and are instantly charmed.

Now, this isn't me taking credit for who my sons are. They deserve all that appreciation for themselves. But I love myself for being able to provide them with an environment where they are free to express themselves, grow into their potential and be as wonderful as they are. And one of the most important things I hope to provide them is the lesson I'm trying to share with you now. I am proud to feel that my sons will be among the lucky children who grow up never doubting that they are worthy of love.

Loving yourself comes when you recognize your own worth without having to hear it from someone else. It's when you take pride in what you know to be true, apart from the judgments others make about you.

I know there are definitely people in my world who aren't convinced my plastic surgery was the right choice. In their minds, the only real way to love myself would be to accept the body I was born with no matter the shape or size. That is very good advice for many people. But you know what? I wanted to change my butt, so I did, and

I'm glad. I didn't do it in the hopes of solving every insecurity I've ever had or achieving some higher level of enlightenment. I wanted a butt lift, and I'm happy I got one. I'm happy I did it for myself, and I'm happy with my butt. Whether or not that helps me love myself is something only I can decide. I'm not going to let other people's negative opinions about what I do with my body interfere with that. Go worry about your own butts.

As I've said, there are countless ways to work toward loving yourself, but it's also important to realize there are countless definitions of what that means. It varies from person to person, and there's no wrong or right answer. Your way of loving yourself might clash with how others around you think it should be done.

But don't let them keep you off of the path that's right for you. Make it your personal superhero mission to stop beating yourself up. Open your eyes to yourself and start seeing all the beautiful things you have to offer the world. At the same time, start working on the things you're unhappy with. A little introspection can go a long way. If you give yourself a chance I guarantee you'll discover all the wonderful things people love about you and you'll start to appreciate them yourself.

Once you open your heart to yourself, you'll start to attract people who respect you for it. The type of people who won't try to suck you into a relationship by preying on your needs. The type of people who will lift you up and treat you with as much love and kindness as you've come to treat yourself. Really take some time every day to appreciate your super strengths, and eventually you'll feel your power starting to grow.

Be Grateful,
But Don't Stop Dreaming

3

Pleasure and pain come naturally. Gratitude takes practice.

In general, we seem to spend more time thinking about the stuff that bring us down than the things that hold us up. We should count our blessings every day. Unfortunately, many of the most valuable things in our lives are things we almost never think about.

For all the time we spend comparing ourselves to other people, you'd think we'd be more blown away by the good things in our lives. If you have a place to live and you don't think that's amazing, you need to take some time to imagine yourself in the shoes of the millions of people around the world who are sleeping on the street tonight.

It's not that you're not allowed to complain. Just because someone else has it worse doesn't mean your problems are invalid. There are few things I hate more than when people dismiss someone's own experiences and feelings by comparing them to some totally different situation. I would hate to do that.

Of course the good things in our lives don't make us immune to pain and sadness. The luckiest girl in the world can still have her heart broken, and she deserves to cry as much as she want without anyone popping in to say, "Hey, at least you don't live in a dumpster."

It's not like I live in a constant state of gratitude. Look at me. I'm publishing a book, something very few people ever get to do, never mind more than once. And you better believe I'll complain about a thing or two before we get to the last page.

But here's the thing. Gratitude isn't an obligation. You shouldn't just try to be grateful because it makes you a better person. You should try to be grateful because it gives you a better life. When you stop to think about the things you take for granted, you're turning up the volume on the good stuff in your life so that it's not drowned out by the bad stuff. And when you practice this kind of gratitude, sometimes you can turn up the good stuff until it's all you hear.

Gratitude is a way to create moments of happiness in spite of whatever is going on in your life. And you know what? Not always, but sometimes, it does have an effect on what you take seriously.

When artists paint pictures, they're always stopping to step back and look at their work from a distance. To get the details just right, the petals of a flower or the eyelashes of a portrait, they have to work close to the canvas. But if they stay zoomed in and focused on that one flower for a long time, they run the risk of making it too bold or too big for the rest of the picture. If they never stepped away to look at the whole thing, they wouldn't be able to keep all the details in harmony.

You see where I'm going with this. When you get hung up on something that's bothering you, it helps to stop and think about how close you are to the canvas. Is the problem really as big as you think it is? Or are you just so focused on it that it's taking up your whole view?

But forget about problems. Gratitude isn't just a way to make yourself feel better. Gratitude *is* happiness. Think about it. What is happiness but gratitude for what we have?

I'm grateful for so many things. My children, my family, my friends. Those are the biggest blessings in my life and the main part of my picture. You can't miss them. I'm thankful for them every single day. It takes more practice to remember the things that are harder to see, the little details that quietly add up to what we call happiness.

I'm grateful that I have a body that lets me run, jump, dance, have children and keep up with them. Not everyone has the freedom of good health, and one day it won't be so easy for me to hop in and out of cars or run up and down stairs without a thought. Whatever body image issues you go through in life, be grateful for what your bones and muscles let you do.

I'm grateful for the fact that I was born in a place where women have the freedom to follow their dreams, get an education and make their own decisions about who to be with and where to live. No one can force me to get married or to stay in a relationship that doesn't make me happy. If you enjoy those basic rights, you're luckier than many women around the world. Every bit of power you have over your own life is something to be grateful for.

I'm grateful for my constant desire to better myself and my life. Statistics are not kind to people with roots like mine. I was born into poverty with an alcoholic single mom who bounced from boyfriend to boyfriend and place to place. I acted up in school, smoked too much weed, had sex too young—the list goes on. Now that I've escaped poverty, addiction and abuse, it would be easy to call it good. But there's something inside me that won't let me settle. Somehow, even though I should have been doomed to the low standards of the life I was born into, there's a passion in me that pushes me to make the most of my life.

I know how lucky I am. I know how good I have it. I know how narrowly I escaped a darker path. And I'm grateful. I practice being grateful every day. And I am thankful for my happiness.

But that doesn't mean I can't be happier. That doesn't mean I can't want more.

Follow Your Heart, But Watch Your Step

4

I know I wouldn't be the first person to tell you that you should always be true to yourself, even when it means going against what other people say. That's one of the biggest clichés there is, and that's because it's good advice. Do what feels right. Trust your gut. Listen to your heart.

But, honestly? Those words should all come with fine print.

I'm not saying they're wrong. If there's one thing I believe in, it's that you should know yourself, love yourself and be faithful to who you really are.

But the fact is, being true to yourself is often the hardest thing you'll ever do.

I know, I know. I set you up to think I was going to say something totally different from what everyone usually says, and then I said another thing you've heard a million times. But stay with me for a second.

When people say it takes strength to be true to yourself, what they're usually talking about is the fact that other people won't always understand. Sometimes, following your heart causes confusion and resistance from the people around you. Especially when what you truly want comes as a shock to them, or goes against what *they* believe is right.

And it's true. That aspect is really, really hard. Being true to yourself often means rejecting the advice of people you trust, and sometimes it even means scaring people who care about you and want you to be happy, but disagree with how to make that happen. It's hard for them and it's hard for you. Because when you're doing what you truly believe is right, there's nothing you want more than to be supported. When all you get instead is disappointment and disapproval, it can truly break your heart.

This is all important to think about, which is why it's smart to say that "being true to yourself" takes courage and strength. But what I'm saying is that there's even more to it than the challenge of going against the grain.

Hustle & Heart

Because even once you get past all the doubts, the judgments, the worries and the arguments from friends and family and everyone else, you might find yourself learning a lesson nobody likes to talk about: sometimes your heart isn't all that great of a leader. A lot of times, it takes you to some shitty places. And *that* can be a hard thing to come to grips with.

"Follow your heart," they say—like your heart already knows the answer, and all you have to do is listen. It's just not true. If it were, life would be so easy! We could all just close our eyes and act on impulse, and everything would turn out great.

But your heart, your gut, your true self, whatever you want to call it, is the deepest part of *you*. It's not like a little wise man living inside you. It's not a treasure chest of perfect answers, or a compass that always points in the right direction.

It's *you*.

You, in your purest form. Not just your desires, but your weaknesses and flaws. So while following your heart is definitely the truest and the most *honest* choice you can make, it's not necessarily one that guarantees smooth sailing.

How well do you know your heart? How would you describe it?

Think about it for a minute.

Now think back to five years ago, or ten years ago. If I asked you the same question, would your answer be the same? Would you expect your heart to make the same decisions?

Or is it possible that it's just as likely to make mistakes as you are?

I'm not trying to bum you out. I promise. And I'm definitely not trying to talk you out of following your heart. Not at all!

I'm saying it's not very wise to assume it will guide you straight to happiness. Hearts are like flashlights. You want to have one in the dark. But if it's not shining bright enough, there's only so much good it can do you.

Growing up, things weren't shining so bright for me. My heart was curious, creative and determined. It was also lonely.

Hustle & Heart

My mom was an alcoholic. So I didn't have the supportive family that the world tells every kid they deserve. Have you ever thought about that? There aren't many things all of society can agree on, but one thing no one will deny is that parents should take care of their kids. Birth parents, adoptive parents, guardians, whatever. Every kid has to depend on somebody, and that somebody is supposed to provide protection, stability and love. Movies, TV, children's books, fairy tales, they all repeat this basic, obvious truth. The world tells kids, "Someone should be taking care of you. You are supposed to be loved."

It's a nice message. But imagine how that message sounds to a kid who isn't taken care of, who doesn't know they're loved. How does that feel? Maybe you don't have to imagine, and you already know. I do. It feels lonely.

And there's no one more vulnerable to disaster than a young person with a lonely heart.

There's a reason we all agree it's so important that kids are loved. Children crave love as badly as they crave food. Maybe even more. Because even though we can "live" without it, our hearts will keep on craving it. And deep inside, in the parts of us where we develop a sense of self, that craving distracts us from dreaming, growing and learning who we are. And if we're not careful, our lonely hearts can lead us down some very unfortunate paths in their desperate attempts to find some way, any way, to be loved.

As far as I could tell growing up, the best of my mom's love went into the bottles she drowned herself in day in and day out. The love that should have been mine went into bottles and empty cans that were tossed in the trash and carried away.

I was left with whatever spilled, and it wasn't enough. Not enough to comfort me when she left me with no one to care for me but a cokehead babysitter. Not enough to numb the embarrassment when she showed up at my elementary school reeking of Jack Daniel's. Not enough to dull my hurt and anger when she disappeared and left me on my own for long, long stretches of time.

By the time I was a teenager, no one had to tell me to follow my heart. With no parent around to tell me what to do, it wasn't even a choice. I ran wild and free with only my heart to guide me. Unfortunately, at that age and under those circumstances, it just wasn't up for the job.

A lot of people have been in this boat. You may be in it right now, living by your own emotions and instincts not just because you're rebellious or stubborn, but because that's truly the only way you know how to keep your head above the waves.

That was me, alone in the ocean, grabbing onto whatever floated my way. My loneliness drove me to lose myself in clouds of weed smoke, in fights that got me suspended from school. And drove me into the arms of boys, where I lost myself in childish fantasies of love.

With no sense of self, not knowing what real love was like or what made a healthy romance, the train went off the rails as soon as it took off. All I wanted was love and stability. Every fiber of me wanted it. I craved it more than anything, and yet year after year, I drifted farther away.

In the eighth grade, I lost my virginity on a sidewalk. At fifteen, I was pressured into sex by a boyfriend who promised to wear a condom, and then took it off without telling me. On my sixteenth birthday, under strong pressure from our parents, I had an abortion.

It shattered me.

For months I was left in a cloud of depression, confused and disappointed by life to an extent no high school sophomore should ever feel.

My heart was trying to lead me to love, but by sixteen it had only sent me down the rockiest and most painful paths.

Bit by bit, I was growing up, starting to examine the feelings inside me that caused me to rush into certain choices, fall into certain situations. I was just beginning to realize that I might never get the love and stability I wanted in the places where I was looking. But you can only grow up so fast. And I was still trying—really trying—to find my footing when, at seventeen, I became pregnant again by my boyfriend Jo.

There was no way in hell I was getting an abortion again. I didn't care who said what about it. I chose to go through with my pregnancy, and I chose to keep the baby. I chose to graduate high school early and start a family with Jo. I chose to sign a contract with MTV, agreeing to appear on the docuseries that, it turned out, would follow the next several years of my life. Most significantly of all, I committed myself to the life of a teen mom.

During my pregnancy, during my relationship with Jo, there were moments of anxiety, uncertainty, fear and doubt. There were impossible sets of choices, where every possible path only guaranteed more uncertainty.

What could I do but listen to my heart? It hadn't kept me out of trouble yet, but it was still my best bet. And slowly, surely, I was finding the strength to be true to myself in a more thoughtful way. Especially once my son Isaac was born, and I finally understood what love was.

All my life I had missed it, craved it, looked for it in the wrong places without ever really knowing what it would feel like. All my life I had just wanted to be loved. But ultimately, it was loving my child that filled that empty space. The pure, unconditional love I felt for my son transformed my world and gave my life a level of meaning and certainty I could never have imagined.

Suddenly, there was much more in my heart than loneliness. My need to be loved shrank down from Godzilla-sized to something much more reasonable. In the space it left behind grew hopes, dreams and ambitions that felt like they had just been waiting for their moment to bloom. I began to see real possibilities around me and form real ideas about the future. My morals and values became clearer and stronger. I started to recognize things I wanted out of life, things I would absolutely never compromise on.

Things had been crumbling with Jo. I wasn't satisfied by the life we were sharing, the constant fights or my growing suspicion that he was cheating on me. One big thing that had been holding me in place was the fact that I had been included in his family. My lifelong desire to feel accepted by a supportive family made it hard to imagine losing his.

But that, too, was the old loneliness talking. And as its influence shrank, that light in my flashlight grew bright enough to guide me to the door.

Hustle & Heart

I believe you'll never be happy if you can't be true to yourself. But you can't be true to yourself without knowing who you are. I believe in listening to your heart, but I also know that a wounded heart gives awful advice.

And that's what no one ever remembers to tell you.

If you were going somewhere dark, would you count on a flickering flashlight? If you were exploring a mountain, would you hire a guide with a broken leg? Would you take a leaky boat out onto the ocean?

It's still true: sometimes the best thing to do is follow your heart. But any time it begins to lead you down some unknown path, remember to watch your step.

You're the Author
of Your Story. Choose the
Characters Wisely.

5

I often get asked how I can cut people out of my life—for example, my mother. In fact, it's often phrased, "How are you able to just cut her out of your life?" *Just*. That one word says quite a bit. How can I *just* cut people out of my life? Like it's no big deal to me? Like I don't care at all?

People are uncomfortable with the idea of someone cutting ties with family, especially parents. The more at peace you are with your decision to distance yourself from a parent, the more it seems to weird them out. Sometimes you can tell they really want to know why you've done it, but they're too polite to ask outright. They'll fish for a hint that something terrible happened. It's like they have an urge to make sure that you're not unfairly shunning your parents, even if they don't know your parents, even if they barely know you.

Other people show sympathy, but it turns condescending. Without even knowing the story or having any idea why you've cut ties, they'll offer cliché advice like, "You should try and work it out." Sometimes they take it upon themselves to remind you that your parent will most likely die before you do, "and you don't want to regret not trying to make peace while you had the chance."

Work it out. Make peace. They say these things like it would be as easy as you and your parent marking a date on a calendar, getting together and letting bygones be bygones. Like it's just an option you're avoiding out of stubbornness and anger. But if you've ever had problems getting along with a parent, you know it's not half that simple.

I admit that I can hold a grudge. I also don't believe you have to forgive someone who has hurt you or done damage to your life. You don't. And you don't have to include people in your life who bring up bad memories or make you feel afraid that they might hurt you again. That's like letting a monster live under your bed because he promises never to grab your ankles. Whether or not he's telling the truth, you'll still be nervous every time you walk by the bed. Even if the monster is a totally reformed citizen, his presence means you'll never really be able to let your guard down.

On the other hand, sometimes you really, really want to let that monster in.

This is why it stings to hear that word, "just." Because I've never *just* decided to cut someone out of my life. The fact that I'm secure in my decision does not mean it was an easy one to make. My refusal to apologize for my choices doesn't mean I feel no pain.

Frankly, it shocks me that so many people don't realize this. It offends me that they feel like they have the right to scrutinize such a delicate, personal, private issue as a child's decision to cut ties with a parent. It hurts when well-meaning people don't realize they're making careless judgments.

You have the right to protect yourself. You have the right to shape your own life. And you have the right to decide what kind of person you want to be.

Here's the thing. The people around you don't just affect your life. They affect who you are as a person, and who you will become.

To love is to accept a person's flaws. Sure. Okay. But what if their flaws affect you in such a way that they begin to warp your inner-self in a negative way?

No one can ever say I didn't try to have a relationship with my mother. I spent the most vulnerable years of my childhood working to hide her drinking from teachers, classmates and neighbors while trying to earn her love. Maybe that made me a devoted daughter.

It also made me a liar. It taught me how to make excuses for someone else's unacceptable behavior. It gave me the impression that my needs were not as important as other people's needs. It taught me to expect very little of someone who was supposed to love me.

This is what happens when you let toxic people stay in your life. Moment by moment, day by day, without even realizing it, you are practicing how to accept not being treated as well as you deserve.

All of these toxic lessons influenced the person I started to become. I was desensitized to things that should have made me uncomfortable, relationships I should have run from, disrespect I shouldn't have tolerated. Desensitized to lies, carelessness and unstable relationships.

That's not the kind of person I want to be. Those are not the values I want to pass down to my children. As a mother, I have a responsibility to instill honesty, integrity and respect in my children. And if anyone undermines that, I won't hesitate to pull that person out of our lives like a weed from the garden.

Happy people, healthy people, *good* people, hold their lives to higher standards. I have every right to do the same.

And so do you.

Never let anyone make you feel high-maintenance for expecting to be treated with honesty and respect.

Never let anyone talk you into compromising the values you hold dear.

Never let anyone tell you that you have to accept mistreatment from someone because they are family.

But, look. In writing, it seems so simple. The logic of it is easy. And yet the decision itself, and living with that decision, is anything but simple and easy.

Cutting ties with a toxic parent may be the best decision you ever make. And yet it will haunt you, because life's a bitch and people judge.

You would expect them to admire the strength and courage that went into your choice. You would expect them to sympathize with the heartbreak that comes with walking away from the one person (or two people) the world promised you that you could count on. You would expect them to know, without asking, that you would never have made this decision if you didn't have your reasons.

But you can't expect any of that. What you can expect is for them to ask you, "How can you just cut people out of your life?" To say, "You should really think about trying to work it out." To say, "You only have one mom" or "one dad." To explain that "Family is family." To remind you that you're in danger of regretting your stubbornness. To tell you that you'll regret your decision.

And when they ask, "What if they die, and you never had a chance to make peace? You don't want to have to live with that." You can expect to get used to a flicker of pain in your heart, because of course you've already thought of that. And they're right. You don't want to have to live with that.

But it's not your fault if you have to. No matter what anyone says.

People who get along with their parents may have a hard time understanding how the rest of us could live without ours. Their parents instilled them with the expectation that parents and kids should love and respect each other, no matter what. Good for them.

Many of us aren't so lucky. But we don't have to settle for the life we're born into. We deserve to have the same standards as those more fortunate.

And if the people in our lives don't make the cut, that's not our fault.

We're the authors of our own lives. We have the power to decide which characters we allow to shape our stories.

And if the critics don't like it, they can read a different book.

True Friends
Encourage You to Grow

6

If you're not born into a good family, you can always make your own.

It would be nice if we were all born to loving and supportive parents, but what can you do? The way I see it, what society calls a happy family is a lot less common than anyone wants to admit. At the end of the day a family is a group of people, a set of relationships and a system of responsibilities. People are complicated, relationships are hard and not everyone can handle responsibility.

Think about what happened in school when the teacher randomly assigned groups for a project. You could work as hard as you wanted and be the best team player in the world, but what really mattered was who you got teamed up with. Even if you didn't land with the class genius and the teacher's pet, you at least hoped for people you could get along with who didn't leave you with all the work. But if you found yourself stuck between the kid who never talked and the girl who bullied you since kindergarten, all you could do was grit your teeth and get through it.

The family I was born into was not a successful group project. My dad was nowhere to be found when I was growing up, and although I tracked him down when I was a teenager, it turned out I felt better leaving him where he was, well outside of my life. My mom was an alcoholic who only saw me through the bottom of her glass. My parents simply were not people who could provide anything remotely resembling a good family.

But it's okay. At least, it is what it is, and it doesn't hold me back now. Whatever I would want from my family, I work to find in my friends. My idea of a family is a group of people who care about each other, are loyal to each other and support each other.

If there's one difference between family and friends, it's that with family there's a stronger guarantee that the relationships will last for your entire life. Although it doesn't always work out that way— parents die or run off or become estranged—there's

Hustle & Heart

an expectation that you'll always have some kind of connection to your mom, your dad, your siblings or your children. Best friends promise the same thing, but the obligation to maintain that bond isn't quite as strong or as reinforced in culture. There's no legal connection, no blood connection and no societal expectation that you'll have some kind of relationship no matter what happens.

Still, even if you believe that good family relationships are deeper and more permanent than good friendships, the fact remains that you can choose your friends. When the most important relationships in your life are your friendships, you don't have to just be randomly grouped with people with no guarantee that they'll be good for you. You can make those decisions. You can look for people who challenge you, support you and inspire you to be your best self, who you trust to step in and help you if you're ever in trouble and who care about your happiness.

As far as I'm concerned, friends are family, and I wouldn't have it any other way. No one gets to be in my life unless I want them in my life. I don't have to reserve space in my world for anyone who doesn't respect it. This is part of keeping my happiness in my own hands.

I know that friends come and go. But whether new or old, I'm glad and proud to know that they bring positivity, encouragement and motivation into my life. There's my friend Sterling, who along with her amazing family has supported me in all of my ideas and projects, investing time, energy and more without ever asking for anything in return. Every time I come out with a book or a T-shirt, they're right there buying it by the dozen and giving it to everyone they know. I didn't exactly have the kind of childhood where my parents pinned my report cards proudly to the refrigerator and bragged about me to their friends. But I don't have to feel bad about it when I have friends like Sterling and her parents cheering me on.

I can't imagine going to my birth family for advice about the things that matter in my life now. But every time I enter some new phase, I've found a friend to share the experience with and turn to for advice and understanding. In college, my friend Tyler has been my right hand at school since the day we met. When I complained to him about filming for *Teen Mom* and said that I wanted to be known for other things outside of that, he just told me to ride the wave until get to where I want to be.

At school I've found friends I can count on for smart, practical advice that's supportive of my goals without any bullshit. That's the kind of stuff I need to hear sometimes. It keeps me going. I haven't known these people all of my life, but we clicked quickly because we have similar levels of drive and focus. We all have goals we're working toward, and we all respect each other's passions.

Recently I went to New York City for about five days to do some work for the show, and my friends from college came to visit. I invited them to come along for the show stuff so that I could introduce them to the producers and other people in the field, giving them a chance to network and maybe build connections for when they grad-uate. It made me feel good that this was something we could enjoy together as a group, that in our friendship, work is something we can all bond over.

During the trip, another group of my friends joined us and they all wanted to go out. I wasn't in the mood, and I had things to do in the morning, but I had a feeling I was going to go along anyway. They had taken the time to meet up in the city, and I didn't want anyone to be upset with me for not being fun. But before I said anything, my school friends spoke up and said I should stay in if I wanted, since they knew I had an early call time in the morning. For them it was a no-brainer that I should worry about my job and my business before worrying about going out late to make someone happy. That was a huge deal to me. I want to be surrounded by people who are positive examples and see the bigger picture. Work now, play later.

Thinking of friends as family means making it a two-way street. When I say I choose friends based on what they bring into my life, I don't want it to sound like I just look for people who will do things for me. Part of what they bring into my life is a belief in mutual respect. They don't just treat me well, they expect me to treat them well, too. In other words, their standards are as high as mine. So one of the most important values they add to my life is that their expectations encourage me to be my best self.

I took a women and feminism class last semester that got me thinking about my responsibility to other women and how we can do our parts to lift each other up. I think one of the best ways is to support each other's ambitions, recognize each other's hard work and encourage each other to higher standards.

People have certain expectations of women. They have certain expectations of men, too. But society's expectations for women, especially wives and mothers, are frustratingly narrow. We're supposed to want certain things, act a certain way and keep certain priorities at the top of our list. And when our behavior doesn't fulfill those expectations, it throws people off. It reads as wrong. Even our friends often struggle to understand what we're doing and worry that we've gone off the rails. Basically, it can be hard for a woman with her own ambitions to find people who support and encourage her.

The original idea for this book came from the part of me that works hard in school, does the best I can as a mother and doesn't settle for less. The last one sometimes gets me called things like bossy, or labeled as a bitch. I have no shame in saying that I'm very forward and I voice my opinion freely. But I don't want to come off as rude or bitchy. I want people to look to me as someone who will do what it takes to get shit done.

When women support each other in going after what they want, we create a well of experience and wisdom that helps us all succeed. By learning through each other, we can get better at navigating the familiar expectations that weigh us down and the obstacles that stand in our way. And we can help each other sort out the weird and confusing challenges we all go through, like spotting the difference between someone offering useful criticism or just subtly trying to tear us down.

I want to tell you something kind of sad. Ever since I was seventeen, I've been reading that I'm only famous for getting knocked up at sixteen, that I only have what I have because of the show, that I'm spoiled by having money I did nothing to deserve. There is a substantial crowd of people out there in the world who go out of their way to tell me that I don't deserve my happiness and that my accomplishments mean nothing. It serves no purpose. There's nothing I could ever do or say to solve the problem they have with me. So there are only two reasons I can think of for why they would make the effort to ridicule me and deny my worth. The first is that they are bullies who find it fun to be mean. The second is that when some people look at me and get the impression that I've worked less than they have but gotten more rewards, it makes them so frustrated and angry at what they see as unfairness that they lash out just to get that feeling out.

I can't do anything for the first type, but I do wish the second type could see that there's more to my life than meets the eye. Yes, being on *Teen Mom* has opened doors for me that I would never have had access to otherwise. But MTV is not a charity foundation. MTV didn't write my books for me. MTV doesn't wake up my husband and me every day to get our kids ready for school and go to work. MTV isn't the reason I get almost all As in school. All of that takes hard work, and I didn't have to do it. I could have treated MTV like a lottery jackpot and ridden the fun train until the money ran out. Instead, I treated it as an opportunity to take my life to a higher level so that I can achieve more for myself, my family and my life after graduation.

I've seen extreme ups and downs, both in the lives of people close to me and in my own. I've struggled before. I've been homeless. I've been on food stamps. I've turned to government assistance to get myself into my first apartment.

Deciding to love myself and learning to be my own support system gave me the strength to believe that I could do better. But it wasn't until I began to confide in positive and successful people that things really started to change for me. It dawned on me that if I only spent time with friends who were unhappy and weren't trying to do better, I would always be stuck where I was. I started looking to people in my life who had college degrees, seeking out knowledge and advice that would help me move onto the next step in life. I asked for help putting together résumés and filling out the necessary paperwork to get loans and grants for school.

People get so distracted by the urge to judge the lives of others that they fail to realize how much good can come from working on themselves. This year I've been trying to prove that's the way to go. I'm trying to be the best me that I can be. And one of the best ways to do that is not to look at other people as competition, but to surround myself with friends I can see as role models.

I wasn't born to parents I could look up to or in an environment that made me aspire to do great things. But I've learned to make up for it with my friends.

Love Should Never
Hold You Back

7

Love is such a powerful word. Just count how many times I use it in this book. There are some relationships in which we use the word habitually, without even really thinking about what it actually means or pausing to feel the genuine emotion behind it as it passes through our lips. There are other times when the word "love" is used as a powerful tool of manipulation. Someone might be thinking of walking out the door, but the moment their romantic partner utters the word "love," they think twice about leaving the scene. They come back.

I'm not a total pessimist, contrary to popular belief. Of course there are those moments when the word "love," in reference to romantic relationships, absolutely holds value and means everything we are told it is supposed to. Passion, intimacy, tenderness and so much more.

What love is *not* meant to be is a tool to hold you in place, or a set of pressures and expectations designed to keep you in the position society says you should be in.

Love should *not* make you complacent. It should *not* make you question yourself. True love should lift you up and make you feel free to explore the world's truths on your own terms.

The person who loves you should always have your back and your best interests at heart. They should do everything in their power to make you feel confident. The perfect relationship is built on unwavering trust and everything should be a positive two-way street.

But that's the so-called perfect relationship, and sure, many of us have experienced the magic of that ideal at some point. In general, however, there are ebbs and flows when it comes to relationships and super intense emotions that inevitably come along with them. Even good love isn't a hundred percent inspiring a hundred percent of the time. It's a challenge to recognize when that percentage is at a normal level versus when it has dipped too low.

Hustle & Heart

One day you may be smitten kittens, and your partner might not be able to keep their hands off of you. This is usually around this same time during the relationship that you can't help but greet him or her at the door looking fab as hell, eagerly waiting for the next moment when you can be wrapped in their arms. A few months later you might be snuggled up on the couch together in sweats, eating too much pizza and arguing over what to watch on Netflix.

There's so much love in both of these scenarios, as long as both people feel they're being respected and they're not giving up some part of themselves to be there.

But let's flip it and reverse it. Maybe you don't feel so keen on greeting your boo at the door, and he or she isn't even inclined to give you so much as a hug. After a long day at work, you might be lucky to get a neutral grunt and a quick hug-and-pat before your partner collapses in exhaustion. And maybe your Netflix quarrels about which show to watch turn into actual fights where suddenly the fact that he likes comedies and you like documentaries spirals into a heated discussion of the differences in your political opinions.

By this point you've probably spent so much time with this person that you've become complacent. You're both generally happy. Generally. I mean, sure, things are tough. Who doesn't have rough patches in their relationships?

It's up to you to take a close and honest look at the big picture of your relationship. Are you going through a temporary situation that will resolve itself when he's done with that big project at work or when you're not dealing with some other anxiety? Are there things going wrong between you that would be easy to fix with a conversation and a change of habits?

More importantly, how is the relationship affecting your happiness? It's one thing when you feel like your relationship is going downhill. But it's even worse when it levels out at a place that's far below where it started. That's when you're in danger of becoming trapped. It doesn't seem bad enough to leave, and it doesn't seem to be getting worse. Sometimes it even gets better for days or weeks at a time. But that doesn't matter when the baseline has dropped below the level that you signed up for.

Love takes work, yes. But there must be rewards for that work. There must be progress. Love should always mean honesty, respect and kindness. But love doesn't mean staying in a relationship that doesn't make you happy anymore. And if your idea of love is stopping you from achieving the level of happiness that you believe you deserve, you need to rethink your understanding of the concept. Because love should never hold you back.

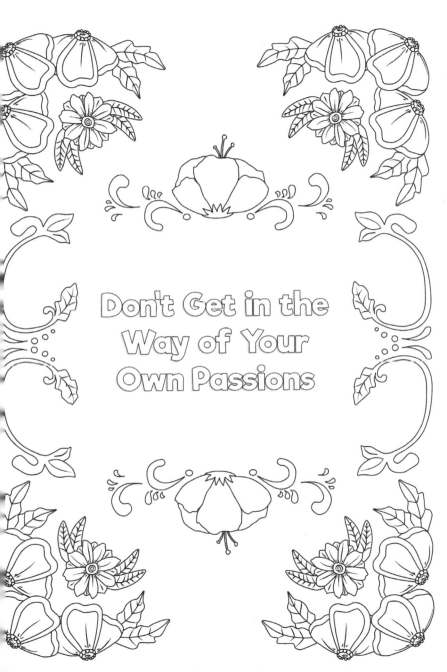

Don't Get in the
Way of Your
Own Passions

8

When I decided to get my Bachelor's degree, I didn't even question that I'd be walking across that stage to accept my diploma in no time. Well, to be specific, in four years. Why would I think any different? That's how long a degree takes. But fast forward to the day when all of my friends and classmates were celebrating the end of the "best four years of their lives," and I was far from finished.

Everyone else was achieving their dreams in the "recommended" time, and there I was with a solid two more years' worth of classwork to accomplish. What was wrong with me? Everyone else had pulled it off. Why couldn't I?

"Kail, you know what you should do?" is a phrase I often hear, followed by unsolicited—albeit well-intentioned—advice. Whether it's friends, family members or strangers on the Internet, everyone seems to have opinions about how they think I should live my life. This goes hand in hand with their thoughts on what, specifically, they think I could be doing better.

I've had people give me "advice" on personal issues ranging from my marriage to my career and everything in between. I know it's not their intention to hurt me or put me down (well, except for some of those haters on social media). But nevertheless, even the most sympathetic advice used to make me feel like they were taking a jab at my accomplishments and all my hard work. It felt like nothing I did was good enough in the eyes of the people around me. I was always coming up short.

Then I made a bold decision. I was going to wash my hands of other people's expectations and focus on the expectations I had for myself. Letting go of the opinions of others and trusting yourself is one of the most courageous things you can do. And let me tell you, while it's not easy, it's given me the confidence to make major life decisions without regret and it's the reason I continue to propel myself forward.

That's not to say the issues I struggle with have magically disappeared. A big part of being able to let go of the peanut gallery and fully trust yourself is the ability to be honest about what you need to work on and then holding yourself accountable for working on those things.

Sounds easy enough, right? Yeah...not so much.

Procrastination is one of the biggest internal battles I've had to face. It's been so bad that at one point I used any excuse in the world just so I didn't have to turn in an eight-page paper— a paper that would put another college credit in my back pocket and move me one step closer to graduating.

A measly eight-page paper. After everything I've been through, it should have been nothing.

Yes, I knew I just needed to roll up my sleeves and do the work. But I found endless reasons to put it off for as long as possible. Being a mom and a student is hard, but trust me—experience had proven that I was completely capable of buckling down and getting it done. If only that pesky demon of procrastination hadn't gotten in the way.

Maybe procrastination doesn't seem like a big deal to you, but chew on this: I've been working on earning my college degree for six years; and no, I'm not studying to become a doctor or a lawyer. Needless to say, I've been inching my way toward graduation for a while.

So, there we have it. I can't do anything but own up to it. I'm Kailyn Lowry, and I'm a procrastinator extraordinaire. You know what they say: the first step to getting better is admitting you have a problem. I've accepted that I have a problem. Now, how am I going to change?

You might be surprised that a lot of people in my life have actually encouraged me to *give up* on earning my degree. Hell, one of my *classmates* even told me we didn't really need the degrees we were working hard at to get jobs in our field. He suggested that I just throw in the towel, what with it taking so long for me and all.

It's not that the thought isn't tempting. Sure, there have been moments when I myself have questioned the decision to stick it out and stay the course. Practically none of my friends work in the field they studied, and despite their higher education, some of them are struggling financially. So, hey. Maybe I should just call it quits and make my life a little easier.

Juggling kids and being on camera while managing a full load of classes often feels like too much. Once, I texted Javi to express how hard it all felt. He texted back, "Hard isn't in your vocabulary. Everything in your life has been hard. A few classes, tests and projects are probably the easiest things you've had to deal with." I have to admit that he's probably right. When I graduate with my Bachelor's degree, I will have defied the statistics of teen mothers. Even more importantly, I'll have accomplished something I always dreamed of.

Now here I am, six years after my first semester, plugging away and more confident than ever that I will earn my degree no matter what. So, how am I going to get there? I'm going to work on my inner battle with procrastination. I'm not going to give up on myself. I'm going to work harder.

"Good things come to those who wait." Easy to say. Difficult to swallow. In theory, this advice is completely reasonable. All you need to do is keep your nose to the grindstone and trust that your hard efforts will pay off when your dreams you've been working for start falling into place.

We live in an instant satisfaction society. By now, we are all used to being able to upload a photo on Instagram and receive hundreds of likes within minutes. We can tweet out a quick question and discover tons of answers immediately. Don't know the definition of a word? Google it. Want to know the song that's playing? Ask Siri. With all of this superficial gratification at the tip of our fingers, it seems like torture when our efforts take longer than expected to pay off. It's even worse to admit that the delay is our own fault.

But goals are meant to push you. Dreams should never be too easy to obtain. Just because life sometimes gets in the way of the perfect plan doesn't mean that your aspirations are any less important, even if they've moved a little ways down the road.

So what if it took me six years to receive my diploma? What matters isn't how long I take. It matters that I get there.

Hustle & Heart

Although these days it's all too easy to get caught up in the moment, it's important to stop and envision your future. You have to remind yourself why you even started doing what you're doing in the first place. I remind myself that earning my degree is about much more than a piece of paper. I'm giving myself the tools necessary to realize my career goals. Of course, I *am* a busy mother of two, so I've often joked that I might take so long to receive my diploma that I'll end up sharing the stage with Isaac or Lincoln some years down the line. If it does take that long, trust that it won't be from procrastination. Life may get in the way, but I won't.

Sometimes Courage
is Letting Go

9

Clearly, I don't give up easily. But this, too, can be a weakness. Of course when you talk about something like struggling to complete a college degree, or persevering to finish off any goal you've invested a ton of time and effort in, you can usually bet that the best advice is to hang in there. Hold on.

But other times, holding on is the worst thing you can do. Sometimes the right thing to do is to let go. And that takes a different kind of courage.

This is never more true than when it comes to ending a relationship with someone you hold dear. I've been through this more than once. I had to do it with my mom, and I had to do it with Jo. And that's definitely not the end of the list.

In both cases—in all cases—what made it hard to let go was the simple fact that I desperately wanted those relationships to work. And the harder I tried to make this wish come true, the more tightly I held on.

You know how it goes. It's one of the oldest traps in the book, and we all fall into it at some point. Once you've invested in something, you don't want to give up on it—even when giving up is obviously the logical idea. It's like ordering a meal at a restaurant and then hating the taste of what's on your plate, but forcing yourself to eat it anyway. You've already agreed to pay for it, after all. So your brain says, "If I don't eat it, I'll have wasted my money." But that doesn't really make sense. Think about it. You have two options: eat a meal that tastes bad, or leave it on your plate. Neither option gets you your money back. Your money is gone. So why make the experience even worse by making yourself eat something you don't like? The only rational thing to do is cut your losses, pass on that gross sandwich and go find some French fries or something.

It's not just money we hate the thought of wasting. We put ourselves through all kinds of unnecessary stress because we've already invested time, or work or love, and we want to stay in it long enough to see that investment pay off. Even if it costs us a little more each day.

I was certainly invested in my relationship with Jo when I caught him cheating on me while I was pregnant. I was so invested that even after that, I was willing to try to find a way to make it work so that I wouldn't have to live with the thought that everything I put into it was all for nothing.

At the end of the day, these relationships weren't meant to be, and even though it was scary in the moment, looking back it was clearly the right choice for me to walk away. That was what was best for our happiness and our lives moving forward.

Letting go is never easy. As much as we want to take Elsa's advice and toss everything we know to the wind, old habits die hard and longtime relationships are difficult to sever.

It's hard to imagine your life without something that has always been familiar. Even if something or someone is doing you more harm than good, change is never easy.

Almost every child grows up fantasizing about some perfect fairytale ending. Fast forward a few years, trade your dream prince or princess for a loving, stable partner, the gorgeous castle for a beautiful home and you've got every romantic's dream. Unfortunately, sooner or later we all must realize that the reality of living this dream is sometimes not what we signed up for.

I'm not saying that even as adults it isn't fun to picture your future with all of your ideal components, but you also have to accept that sometimes Prince or Princess Charming doesn't come to rescue you from your castle.

I thought I had my fairytale ending on September 4, 2012—the day I said "I do." I had Javi, my knight in shining armor, and we had big plans to build a castle together where we'd raise our children in a stable, two-parent home. We welcomed Lincoln into our family just over a year after we took our vows and we couldn't have been happier. All of our dreams were coming true. We were well on our way to having it all.

Hustle & Heart

Fast forward a year or two down the road and my relationship was far from the fable I'd imagined my life would be with Javi. We decided the best course of action to work on our relationship would be to enroll in couple's therapy to try to mend our issues. For a while things seemed to be getting better, but there were underlying problems that always seemed to sneak up on us even when it felt like we were doing everything we could to make our relationship stronger. It always felt like we were going two steps forward, one step back. Or was it two steps forward, three steps back? Every day was so different that at a certain point I didn't know if we'd ever come out in front.

So what went wrong? There wasn't some huge fight or scandal. What took a toll on our relationship was a perfect storm of different things, both big and small.

I'm very ambitious when it comes to achieving my career goals, and while I'm not a hundred percent sure just yet what I'll end up doing in the future, I have a lot of business ideas. Not too long ago, there was one in particular I was extremely excited about. I had decided that I wanted to open a blowdry bar, an idea my friends were so supportive of that I actually hired someone to help me write a thirty-four page business plan to present to my bank in order to get a loan.

Everything was going swimmingly. The research I'd done had presented me with numbers that looked very promising. I was confident I could get this business off the ground and it would be successful. I was beyond excited at the thought of this particular dream coming to fruition. Javi, on the other hand, was not on board. In fact, he was downright unsupportive, knocking down the idea every time I brought it up.

With each jab, unsupportive remark or put-down, my enthusiasm for moving forward with the blowdry bar started to wane until eventually I completely lost all my steam. I was deflated. How could my own husband not have my back? It stung. If anyone in life should be your number one fan—beside yourself—it's your partner. It was starting to feel less and less like we were a team.

Hustle & Heart

The feeling that I was losing my teammate only grew stronger when Javi started to become controlling and jealous. When he did things like demanding that I unlock my phone to prove I had nothing to hide, or calling me constantly when I was enjoying time with friends to make sure I wasn't doing anything "sneaky" behind his back, it became clearer and clearer how little my husband trusted me. I had done nothing to make him doubt me. I never lied, never went behind his back and I was never unfaithful. For some reason, he was convinced otherwise. Naturally, this caused a lot of fights and arguments.

As we struggled to keep our relationship afloat, our number one priority was our children. The last thing we wanted was for our unhappy marriage to affect them. As a married couple we were forced to ask ourselves if we should stay together for the kids, or if it would be better for them if we ended things amicably and co-parented.

At the beginning of our marriage I never in a million years imagined divorce was something Javi and I might face. How did our fairytale fall apart? Maybe we needed to do more couple's therapy. Or maybe, as scary as it was to think, it was time to get courageous and let go...no matter how much it broke my heart.

It was agonizing to think about what the outcome would be if Javi and I ultimately decided that divorce was the best option for our relationship. It would mean Lincoln growing up without mom and dad together under one roof. Just like Isaac. It would mean my dream of raising my kids in a two-parent home would go by the wayside.

But if you remember, my goal was always to raise my kids in a *stable, happy* home. Maybe that wasn't something that Javi and I could provide for them together anymore.

I finally realized that whether Javi and I stayed together or split apart, there was no question that my children would never be without a stable, happy home. There just might be more than one.

Be Your Own Support System

10

Growing up, I had the bare minimum of a support system. I'd even venture to say I had none at all. My dad was nowhere to be found while I was helping mom make excuses and cover up her alcoholism. It was during this time that my mom kept dragging me from town to town with her boyfriend du jour.

As you can imagine, this made it increasingly difficult for me to make and maintain deep, genuine friendships at school. In my "household" there was no structure, no boundaries, and what felt to me like no love. Living this way forced me to grow up faster than your average kid. Not only did it send me into a spiral of using pot and sex to overcome my feelings of abandonment, but over the years this lack of support weighed on me more than I even understood at the time. It tugged at my heart. All I wanted was to feel loved and taken care of. It affected me so profoundly that it clouded my judgment.

I found myself with a death grip on anything that felt remotely like love and solace. On the surface these types of relationships felt good, fuzzy and warm. I wanted to hold onto them as tightly as I could, but deep down I think I knew that these were illusions.

But it took a very long time for me to learn the real truth: if I was ever going to find the love and stability I was looking for, it would have to come from me. I needed to be my own support system.

I had wild expectations about the people in my life, expectations they were never quite able to live up to. It's a hard life lesson to learn, but you have to manage your expectations of others and be prepared to deal with the fact that some people might straight up let you down. That's something we're not typically prepared for but it happens all too often.

That's why it's important to recognize that you and you alone are your best and most reliable support system. Throughout my life I've chased so many support systems to make up for feeling neglected as a child. When Jo and I started dating, I was amazed by his seemingly perfect home life. He had a stable home with two loving parents and an extended family that never missed a holiday, birthday or graduation.

While a big happy family was completely alien to me, it was also everything I had ever wanted. You can imagine my shock when Jo and I decided to tell his extended family about my pregnancy at Jo's graduation, and their reactions were positive. They were supportive. I couldn't believe how lucky I was to have been to be accepted into such a kind and caring family. Being seventeen and pregnant was obviously not an ideal situation, but they showed us nothing but love. They realized we were two scared kids who were about to become parents, an undertaking many fully formed adults struggle with.

I put off sharing the news with my mom for as long I possibly could but as my belly grew and my due date got closer I had no choice but to tell her the real reason I was throwing up every morning.

In my dream world filled with high expectations I held out hope that news of becoming a grand-mother would motivate my mom to make major changes in her life and overcome her addictions. I wished this would push her to transform into the loving supportive mother I'd wanted all my life. Instead, there was no support and certainly no transformation.

They say when people show you who you are you should believe them. My mom had showed me her true colors for my entire life, yet it still felt like a major blow to have zero support from her during this terrifying time in my life. Luckily, Jo's mom and dad had started making arrangements for Jo and I to move into their basement. When it finally came time to make the move, my mom signed custody of me over to Jo's parents. Just like that, I had what felt like a real family. The very thing I had been craving for as long as I could remember. The ultimate support system.

The thing about relying on others for support is that it can force you to get stuck in unhealthy rela-tionships and patterns. I stayed with Jo much longer than I should have because I couldn't imagine reverting back to a life without outside support. I was crushed at the thought of losing Jo's family, which made breaking up Jo that much harder.

When all was said and done, I was on my own once again.

As I worked through the pain of losing the only support system I'd ever known, I finally realized what I had been failing to see all along. I needed to be my own support system. Sure, I had tons of wonderful, loving friends, but being my own cheerleader was the best way to protect myself from allowing anyone to let me down. Being a single mom was going to be the hardest thing I'd ever done, and I wasn't about to let anyone make it that much harder by giving me false hopes and then tearing the rug out from under me.

Becoming your own support system is much easier said than done. We all want people in our lives who are there for us no matter what, to help pick up the pieces when we we're falling apart.

When Javi and I got married his family and friends welcomed me with open arms. Once again

I had the support system I had wanted for so long, but this time something was different. I was different. No matter what the future held, I knew I would be just fine whether I had someone to lean on or not. If I was left on my own again, I knew I could hold myself up.

By then I'd been through hell and back. I'd watched friends come and go. I'd been let down more than you can imagine. These experiences helped me manage my expectations of others. They made me learn not to fear the thought of taking care of myself. Because the fact is, even if it's easier to have someone else drive you around, you should always know that you can get back in the driver's seat and get yourself where you need to go.

Take Pride in
What You've Survived

11

Every generation comes with changes in the way we talk about this or that issue. Things that used to be okay are suddenly frowned upon. Words go out of style. New ones are invented. We start to question things we took for granted. We start to fight back against things our parents and grandparents thought they couldn't change.

For this generation, one of those things is sexual assault. The way we talk about it now is completely different from the way it was just a few years ago. It's even changed since I was a teenager. Rape is a hot topic, and not just the old-fashioned idea of being violently attacked in an alley. People, especially women, are starting to speak out about what it's like to feel trapped in an unwanted sexual situation or be pressured into doing something after very clearly resisting.

Now that I'm older, it's interesting to hear these new discussions in the background as I naturally think back to my own experiences. Like most people, I've had sex when I didn't want to have sex. Sometimes lines were blurry. Sometimes they weren't at all. But I can't help wishing these conversations had been happening back then. Maybe I wouldn't have felt like I had to get over it all on my own.

One night in the ninth grade, my boyfriend surprised me by pressuring me into sex. Toby and I had been together for two years, on and off. He was a popular guy with tons of friends. He also had a dark mess of feelings thanks to the fact that his mother and father had recently split up. Everyone's always working through something. When Toby asked me to hang out for the night at his place while his parents were out, I went.

It wasn't just us. His friend was there, being irritating. The minute I walked in the door, the friend started making fun of Toby about the fact that he and I hadn't had sex. I didn't like it. And as Toby leaned into the peer pressure, spiraling into stereotypical bullshit boy behavior with his friend, I felt more and more cut out of the party. But as annoying as it was, I couldn't complain about his buddy's presence. I didn't want Toby to think I'd come over to be alone with him, and take that as a message that I wanted to have sex.

But his friend left, and Toby took me by the hand. "Let's have a baby," he said, "so we can be together forever." I was caught off guard and completely horrified. It made no sense. But suddenly Toby seemed to be on a mission. He wouldn't take no for an answer.

The events that followed are blurry in my memory. But I remember clearly that I didn't want to sleep with Toby. There was no doubt about it. But he persisted. And I gave in. I believed he loved me, and I didn't have the heart to fight against giving him what he seemed to want so badly.

My only condition was that he wear a condom. He did. But guess what? He took it off. I didn't know until it was over. And he didn't care. Until I told him I was pregnant.

Later, my mom called it rape. I wasn't ready for that word. How could I commit to a word that sounded so big, with a definition so controversial people can't even decide on it? Even as time went on and I got a better understanding of how grave the situation was, that concept remained intimidating.

Years later, after having a child, a guy who'd been asking me out for awhile showed up at my apartment plastered. He said he needed to talk to me. I let him in. He grabbed me, dragged me into the bedroom and forced me down. I said stop and tried to fight, but he was too strong—and too rough. I bled. I screamed. And when he left me, my body torn and my sheets stained with blood, I felt like I was dead.

At the hospital the doctors stitched me up. The pain was unbearable. It was obvious what had happened to me. And yet I wouldn't agree to a rape kit. I was shaken and afraid and overwhelmed by chaotic ideas of what would happen if I accused Caleb of rape. I couldn't stand to think about the consequences.

People have strong opinions now about rape and sexual assault. Survivors are getting braver about sharing their experiences and even calling out their accusers. We've come up with new terms and phrases that help us fight back against the systems that silence victims and the cultural codes that protect offenders. We've started to talk about what consent means. People are starting to resist the tendency to blame victims for what happens to them.

It's nice to see that kind of social progress. But when you're assaulted, you feel far away from it. There's only you, your memories and your shame. And you cope with it any way you can.

Some people judge me for not going to the police. Maybe they think I'm a coward. I felt like one sometimes. I would have preferred to be a hero, to avenge myself, to smack down my rapist by bringing him to justice. I would like to have been the ideal survivor. But I wasn't. I blamed myself for what had happened. I refrained from telling anyone. And even as it ate away at me, I tried to pretend it had never happened. I tried to escape into a reality in which I wasn't a victim.

When I look back now, it's hard to accept that I wasn't the badass survivor I would have hoped to be. If only I had stood up for myself, raised my voice and backed up my beliefs. If only I'd been living proof of the fact that no victim should live in shame. Then I could have turned what happened into a source of strength. I could be looking back now and feeling proud of myself.

But I am proud of myself. Because I managed to move forward. I didn't let those experiences define me forever. Slowly, piece by piece, I recovered my confidence and stepped out of the shadow of sexual assault.

I'm proud of myself for surviving.

I never want anyone to feel like I did, to be too afraid and ashamed to even admit what happened to them. My greatest hope is for victims to raise their voices, speak their truths and hold their abusers accountable for their crimes. Speaking out about sexual assault, rape and abuse is a brave and beautiful thing to do.

But everyone handles trauma in different ways. It's okay if you're not an inspirational example, if you don't fit the description of a perfect survivor. You deserve just as much admiration and respect as those people who raise the battle cry. Because you survived one of the most devastating experiences anyone can ever go through, and you went on to face another day.

As a survivor, every happy moment you experience after your trauma is a victory—whether people know it or not. Whatever your experience and however you cope, try to take pride. You may feel like no one sees how hard you're trying every day, how far you've come or what you've accomplished. But there are people out there who understand. I do. And I want you to know that you're amazing, I admire you and you deserve to be proud.

This One's for the Boys

12

How do I even begin to express how it feels to be the mother of Isaac and Lincoln? My two guys are everything to me, and there aren't enough words in the world for me to truly convey how full my heart feels every time I hear them laugh or experience those beautiful moments when I'm bombarded with kisses. There's truly nothing better than watching them grow (even if it does happen so fast it's scary), or when I get to be there as they discover something new and exciting about life.

By now we've established that when I was a kid my dad was completely out of the picture, and although my mom was technically around, she was less than "present." Frankly, neither of my parents was capable of enjoying all the amazing gifts that come with being a parent.

When I was younger, I used to feel sorry for myself for everything that I missed out on thanks to their shortcomings as parents. But now that I'm a mom myself, sometimes I almost feel sorrier for them. Once you've experienced the joy that comes with embracing your role as a parent and helping your children thrive, your perspective changes forever. It's hard for me to understand how anyone can be so close to that miracle yet miss it. My parents really missed out.

That's why I feel so grateful for Javi, Jo, Vee and all of the amazing family and friends that my kids and I are so lucky to have in our lives. A strong community of loving, supportive people is everything I've ever wanted for my children, and this particular community of people never ceases to amaze me with the ways they always go above and beyond.

Sure, kids are always shaking parents down for the latest toy, or let's face it, in 2016, the newest tech gadget. "One more story!" they'll say as they're snuggled up in bed looking up at you with those gorgeous doe eyes you can't help but resist. "Just a little bit more screen time?" they'll ask when they see you reaching for the remote or for their iPad.

"Mom, is dinner ready yet?" they'll ask on repeat until a nice home-cooked meal is sitting in front of them on the table. Then they'll barter with you about how many veggies they have to eat to be "done."

I might be exasperated or exhausted beyond belief when fielding these types of questions and requests. If I say no and someone's cranky, a tantrum might ensue. Are these moments hard? Hell, yes. But I see all of them as blessings. I know that might sound weird, but hear me out.

When I was kid I didn't have time to think about toys or TV time. There was no stalling for just one more bedtime story, because there were no bedtime stories. If I wanted a home-cooked meal, there was no one there to make it for me. I would have to make it for myself. You could say I grew up too fast, but it's actually even worse, if you ask me. I was still a kid. I just didn't have anyone grown-up around me.

All good parents will tell you that they want to give their children all the things they never had growing up. To some, this might mean elaborate holidays and birthdays filled with gifts. To others, it might mean a better education. There are all kinds of things we want to give our kids. For me, the most important thing I want to give my children is a childhood.

Due to the lack of parenting in my childhood, I had to take on so many adult responsibilities that it blows my mind to this day. That's why it's my mission as a mother to make sure my children grow up at the right pace, and are never confused about who is the parent and who is the child. My kids will never doubt that they're loved unconditionally, and I'll do everything in my power to give them all the tools they need to be their best selves.

This next section might embarrass Isaac and Lincoln later in life. Sorry buddies! But this one's for you. Because there's a lot of advice that I wish my mom had given me as a kid. And this is my choice to impart that on you now.

Get messy.

Yes, you have my permission. Don't be afraid to roll around in the grass. Finger paint with reckless abandon. Just not on my walls, please, if you can help it. Let ice cream melt all over your face, shirt and shoes. Enjoy every moment of the mess. When you get older, life will inevitably get messy in different ways. They won't be as fun, but that's okay. I won't judge you for making a mess, and I'll be there to offer you the guidance and support it takes to get you through it.

Explore.

The world is yours to explore. Don't be afraid to go down different paths and try new things. Not everything you try will be your cup of tea, but don't give up on jumping into new experiences. Keep searching. When you find something you feel passionate about, dive into it head first. You never know where it may take you.

Don't be afraid to take chances.

A lot of things in life are scary, especially those moments when you can't tell where any of the paths around you will lead. But don't let that stop you from taking chances. You might not always succeed. In fact, you're bound to fail. But that's part of life. Just know that I will always be there. As long as you are true to yourself and respectful of others, I'll never judge you for taking a risk to follow your dreams or embark on an adventure. I'll always have your back. From scraped knees to a broken hearts, I'll be right by your side.

Guard your heart, but always be kind.

Life is full of good and bad. We need the bad things to make us appreciate the good. But even knowing that pain and disappointment are natural parts of life, I still wish I could wrap you in my arms and protect you from it all. Unfortunately, you won't always fit in my arms, and even the best parent in the world can't shield their kids from getting hurt. Nor should they. My job is to give you the confidence and integrity to fight through your own challenges and come out on the right side. In the meantime, the best thing I can do is to impart you with this advice: guard your heart. Be cautious of who you let in. Now, this advice has your mom written all over it, and I'll be truthful and tell you that not everyone will like that I'm giving it to you. But my realism has given me strength and conviction in life, and has helped me succeed. So I'm sharing it with you. Be careful who you let in. Take your time in deciding who to trust. Let your relationships develop slowly and naturally. And when you do feel confident that you've found someone who won't let you down, whether it's a friend or a partner, don't let them go. You may get a lot of good out of people who come in and out of your life bringing fun, excitement and novelty. But pay special attention to the ones who you can count on to be in it with you for the long run.

Take care of each other.

Both of you have been blessed with the gift of a sibling. The bond you will share with your sibling throughout your life is sacred. There will certainly be times when it doesn't feel this way. Most likely when you are teenagers, which, trust me, I am already bracing myself for. If you're like any other set of brothers in the world, there will be times when you will fight and tease one another.

You might compete with each other. Tears may be shed and feelings may be hurt. But no matter how many squabbles or arguments there are between you, you will always share a special bond with your sibling. I've watched it form before my eyes. Years and years down the line, you'll be the only ones who share the memories of these early years you spent together. You'll be the only ones who've seen each other cry in the backseat of a car while your mom tried to keep her sanity in the front. These special experiences and this special knowledge of each other is why you will always be capable of being each other's nearest and dearest friend. Besides your mom and dad, there will be no one else in your life who has known you longer or better, and between the two of you there is a bond and an understanding that even your parents can't compete with. No matter where life takes you, you'll always have each other.

I believe in you.

I believe in you. Plain and simple. My belief in you is unwavering. There isn't a mistake in the world you can make that will ever make me give up on you. I have known you and loved you since you were just little specks inside of me. I have watched you grow and felt more pride in you every day. I know that life will throw difficulties at you, and that I won't always be able to fix them for you. I know you'll take on challenges that you'll need to conquer on your own. I know you'll have times of doubt, times when you're not sure who you are, and times when you worry about how you're doing on this crazy journey called life. And I won't always have the answers for you, but I will give you one truth that will never change. I love you, I have always loved you and I will always love you just the way you are. Never, ever doubt how much I believe in you.

Don't Fear the Future.
It's Going to Happen Anyway.

13

Change is scary. So is the unknown. Like any other creature on earth, all we want as humans is a safe place to live and grow. In our minds, we dream of thriving. In reality, we settle for living. And once we put down a few roots somewhere, we lose sight of the difference.

We start to think, isn't living enough? How much better could it be somewhere else? How much are we missing if we stay? What could we lose if we leave?

How should we decide what's enough for us? How do we find a balance between gratitude and ambition? Clearly we all have different standards. A person raised in wealth and comfort expects more out of life than a person raised in poverty and violence.

Someone who is used to having less will be satisfied with less. But do they have to be? What should we be content with?

Are food, water and shelter enough to be happy? As long as we have a roof over our heads, are we allowed to dream of a nicer house? As long as we're not hungry, is it wrong to crave wine and cookies once in awhile?

And how about marriage? Is it enough not to hit each other, not to lie, not to cheat? Is it enough to love each other, steadily and safely? Or should there also be passion? Should there be excitement?

When one person's idea of luxury is another person's bare minimum, how can you be sure if you're asking for too much or not enough? What happens when the things that satisfy everyone around you leave you wanting more?

For some people who have only ever been with lied to by their partners, an honest relationship would be a dream come true. If they had someone like that, they think, they would never let go.

For those who grew up with parents who were passionately in love, respect and honesty may not be enough to keep them in a relationship. As far as they know, a truly healthy relationship requires adventure, laughter and excitement.

Hustle & Heart

For many who grew up with violence, a quiet and peaceful house might be all they'll ever dare to dream of.

Who is to say where you should set your standards? Who has the right to tell you they're too high?

We're told to reach for the stars, to chase our dreams. But when everyone around you seems satisfied with what they have, suddenly you feel crazy for wanting more. It's like everyone decided the journey was over, when you know beyond a doubt that your destination is still ahead. They like this spot. They don't see why you wouldn't be happy to settle down. They don't get why you would want to keep going or what you think you're going to find.

It feels wrong to say that what's good enough for them isn't good enough for you. And you start to wonder if maybe you *are* wrong. Maybe you *are* crazy for wanting more. Maybe the difference between living and thriving isn't as big as you think. Maybe you are thriving, and you're just not letting yourself see it. Maybe it *doesn't* get better than this.

Or, there's a simpler answer: maybe what's right for others isn't right for you. And maybe, just maybe, it's time you made peace with that.

It's scary to leave a safe place to go out and look for something better. Most people won't do it. They're afraid they won't find what they're dreaming of, and they won't be able to return to what they had.

Sure, on the surface it seems like the smartest thing is to stay in one place. Why risk a big change?

But the reality is that there's no such thing as staying in one place. Life moves forward no matter what we do, and things change no matter what. You might think that by staying where you are, you can hold onto your current situation forever. But in five years, ten years, fifty years, there's no telling what this same place will look like or feel like. Years from now it could be completely unrecognizable. What excites you today could bore you to misery down the road.

If you're not satisfied with the situation you're in, staying put is just as risky as moving on. You can't predict the future either way. And you shouldn't trick yourself into thinking you can avoid it.

Hustle & Heart

At some point in your life, you've probably taken a risk when you could have played it safe. What if you had made a different choice at the last fork in the road? Can you be sure of what your life would look like now? Absolutely sure? Or isn't the "safe route" just as hard to predict?

When you've already achieved more than you ever thought possible, it's a bold move to ask for more.

But maybe that's what "hustle and heart" really means.

The audacity to aim higher than you're supposed to.

The strength to take your happiness into your own hands.

The ability to embrace change.

The courage to face the future.

I don't know where I'll be a few years from now. But my heart is telling me I'm not done with my journey.

So I guess I'd better hustle.

Afterword

Since I've written *Hustle and Heart,* a lot has changed. I've traveled a lot, learned even more, and I finally came to terms with the fact that Javi and I should no longer be together. We're getting a divorce, and I'm okay with that now.

The thing I've always been concerned about is how my separation from Javi would affect Isaac and Lincoln. Isaac calls Javi "dad," and Lincoln is very attached to his father. My focus became so intent on trying to make my marriage work that I forgot how Lincoln and Isaac were seeing me from their viewpoint. They were seeing a mom that was moody, confused, and unhappy. How could I raise healthy kids if I wasn't healthy myself?

Then I realized that one unhappy house is much worse than two happy ones. I want my children to feel loved every day, and it doesn't matter if that comes from divorced parents or not. I want my kids to learn how to be strong and make decisions that make them a better person. I know this is what's right for me, and Isaac and Lincoln know their mom is happier and independent. Jo and I repaired our relationship for Isaac's sake, and Javi and I will do the same.

I so appreciate Javi and the love we shared while it lasted. He's a hard worker and a good father. We made some great memories and created a warm and welcoming home together. But right now, I have to focus on myself and being the best mom I can be. I'm not perfect and never will be. I'm just growing up and maturing and learning what is most important.

It's even harder to go through these things in the public eye, with people judging your every move. Hearing the awful things that people who have never met me say about me and my relationship has taught me the biggest lesson in all of this: I know now what kind of person and friend I want to be. If any of my married friends go through something similar, I want to stay completely out of their business. I want to only provide them with positive advice and be supportive in whatever they decide to do.

Everyone needs a supportive team behind them. For me, it's been my friends. They've reminded me to be positive and be content with the decision I've made. They tell me to be grateful for how far I've come, and that I'm beating the odds by staying in college. When I'm feeling down, they encourage me to look at Isaac and Lincoln and feel proud. Isaac is so smart and kind to everyone he meets, and Lincoln is so sweet and makes me laugh every day. They are my biggest accomplishments.

Change happens. I've changed from the beginning of this book to the end, for the better. But one thing will never change: the love I have for my kids. I will always strive to make the best choices I can for them, even if they're hard as hell. I've dedicated my life to making theirs better than mine was. Whatever it takes, I'm doing it.